THE TRUTH BEHIND
SNACK
FOODS

JULIA J. QUINLAN AND ADAM FURGANG

To Caleb, who loves to snack on grapes and strawberries —AF

Published in 2018 by The Rosen Publishing Group, Inc.
29 East 21st Street, New York, NY 10010

First Edition

Library of Congress Cataloging-in-Publication Data

Names: Quinlan, Julia J., author. | Furgang, Adam, author.
Title: The truth behind snack foods / Julia J. Quinlan and Adam Furgang.
Description: New York : Rosen Central, 2018. | Series: From factory to table : what you're really eating | Includes bibliographical references and index. | Audience: Grades 5–8.
Identifiers: LCCN 2017020260| ISBN 9781499439366 (library bound) | ISBN 9781499439342 (pbk.) | ISBN 9781499439359 (6 pack)
Subjects: LCSH: Food—Composition—Juvenile literature. | Snack foods—Juvenile literature. | Junk food—Heath aspects—Juvenile literature.
Classification: LCC TX551 .Q58 2018 | DDC 664/.07—dc23
LC record available at https://lccn.loc.gov/2017020260

Manufactured in China

CONTENTS

The snack food aisle in the grocery store is packed full of brightly colored, packaged options in just about any flavor or texture you could want. Bite-sized cookies, chips, popcorns, flavored nuts, candy, and so on. It's not just in grocery stores that you find these snacks. They're in convenience stores, vending machines, and even department stores. The checkout counters of many stores have a selection of grab and go snacks. You never have to worry about being hungry; there's always a snack somewhere that you can pick up.

This may sound wonderful and convenient, but the overconsumption of snack foods is having a serious effect on people's health. Packaged, highly processed snack foods are often full of sugars and sodium. The prevalence of snack foods is throwing people off of the traditional three-meals-a-day way of eating. When you have some chocolate chip cookies between breakfast and lunch, some cheesy popcorn between lunch and dinner, and some sour candy after dinner, you've pretty much eaten a whole extra meal! Not to mention all of the preservatives, additives, sugar, and sodium you've taken in.

These snacks may seem small individually but the problem is that many people are not just having a sugary or salty snack once in a while. They've become a regular part of many people's diets. Between the 1970s and the 1990s, salty snack food consumption more than doubled in the United States. The consumption of sugary snacks increased dramatically during this time, too.

Of course, sugar and salt, or sodium, are things that the human body requires to function normally. However, the amount that most people consume is

Salty snacks are very tasty, but they should be eaten in moderation. Too much salt is not good for the body.

far more than the body needs. Too much salt and sugar can have serious short- and long-term health effects.

It is hard to avoid these snacks as they seem to pop up wherever you turn! That is on purpose. The snack food industry spends an enormous amount of money on advertising and marketing. They want to make their snack food seem like the most delicious and the coolest. Much of this marketing is aimed at kids.

It is important to think critically about what you're eating and why you're eating it. Are you eating that snack food because you are really hungry or because your favorite pop star is a spokesperson for it? How much sugar do you really need in a day? Why are those chips bright orange?

Being in control of your own mind, body, and choices are an essential part of a healthy life. Sugary and salty snacks should not be eaten regularly. There are plenty of natural, unprocessed, and filling snacks available that provide energy and nutrients.

CHAPTER ONE

SALT AND SUGAR OVERLOAD

Y ou would never just eat tablespoons of sugar, but with today's snacks, you're doing just that! Today, many processed snacks have way too much sugar and salt, and they are hiding in plain sight, listed right on the ingredient labels. This includes many snack foods that are considered "healthy," such as breakfast bars, energy bars, canned soup, and whole wheat breads.

In order to function properly, the body needs a large variety of nutrients from many sources, including sugar and salt. It is natural to crave them. But the foods in our grocery stores make these ingredients far too easy to come by, so we tend to get much more of them than our bodies require.

Today, snacks are manufactured on a huge scale and delivered all around the globe. Our love for tasty snacks has led to

Nutrition Facts		
Potato chips, salted		
Serving Size 100g/3.5oz		
Amount		% Daily Value
Calories 522		
Calories from Fat 330		
Total Fat 34 g		55%
Saturated Fat 9 g		54%
Trans Fat		0%
Cholesterol 0 mg		22%
Sodium 540 mg		18%
Carbohydrate 51 g		18%
Fiber 5 g		0%
Sugars 0 g		31%
Protein 5 g		2%
Vitamin A		
Vitamin C		

This is a typical nutrition facts label. Familiarizing yourself with these labels is a great way to know what you're eating.

an increase in food production and has caused the manufacturing industry to work more efficiently. As with any business, snack companies are constantly trying to decrease production costs, so they have come up with ways to save money. One way is to produce more goods at once. Another way is to create new ingredients that allow food to be made cheaply and increase the shelf life of these foods. As a result, snack foods are more commonplace and more processed now than ever. You don't have to go very far to satisfy your craving for sugar or salt.

The ingredients in your foods may shock you. One such ingredient is high-fructose corn syrup. This artificial sweetener is

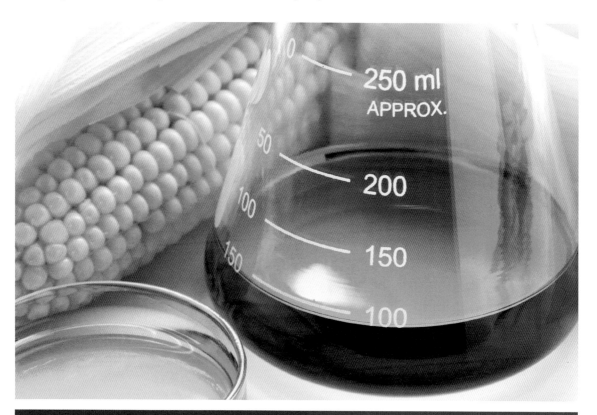

High-fructose corn syrup starts out as corn, but it's made in a laboratory.

manufactured from corn and has become so cheap to make that it is now put into sugary snack foods in alarmingly high quantities. More and more studies have linked overconsumption of this now common ingredient to many health problems. To be a healthy and informed consumer, it helps to know what is going into your foods.

SUGARS AND SWEETENERS

Pure sugar is an organic compound that has a very high calorie content. Our bodies convert these calories into energy or store them as fat faster than anything else we consume. Traditionally, naturally sugar-rich foods, such as berries and other fruits, only grow in their natural environments once a year, when they are in season. Our bodies have evolved to savor and crave these foods so that we were sure to get their nutrients when the food is available and to help store fat for when it was not. Pure table sugar comes from sugar cane, a plant that grows in warm climates like South America. Other natural sugars also come from honey and maple tree syrup. Today, you could be on any continent in the world at any time of the year and easily find a sugary treat.

You might have a hard time finding old-fashioned sugar listed as an ingredient in your snack foods today, but don't let that fool you. There are now about forty different kinds of sweeteners in modern snack foods. The list of processed sugars is hidden in plain sight on food labels. They are disguised with names such as high-fructose corn syrup, barley malt, dextrose, modified corn starch, beet sugar, fructose, sucrose, brown rice syrup, malt, sorbitol, invert sugar, fruit juice concentrate, galactose, lactose, polydextrose, turbinado sugar, mannitol, xylitol, and maltodextrin.

Seeing all those terms for sugar is enough to make your head spin. Many people do not even know what most of these words mean and just consume their snacks without thinking about it, never realizing that they're all forms of sugar and adds unnecessary calories and weight to our bodies. It has now been shown in studies that our bodies metabolize fructose differently from other sweeteners, and too much of it can affect the liver similarly to the way too much alcohol can. Rates of obesity increased in the United States not long after industry grade high-fructose corn syrup was mass-produced in the 1980s. It is now a common ingredient in thousands of snacks.

Do you think you get the right amount of sugar in your diet? Let's find out. The US Food and Drug Administration (USDA),

Here, you can see sugar cane growing in a field. Sugar comes from plants. Artificial sweeteners come from a lab.

recommends no more than twenty-five grams per day for women and no for than thirty-seven grams per day for men. Four grams of sugar is equal to one teaspoon of sugar, so forty grams equals ten teaspoons of sugar. If that sounds like a lot, consider that one twenty-ounce bottle of typical fruit punch can have the equivalent of eighteen teaspoons of sugar! And most of the time, its not even pure sugar, but rather chemical imitations created in a lab.

It doesn't end there. A single serving of a chocolate candy bar can have as many as twenty-five grams of sugar. Red licorice can have forty-two grams of sugar per serving. Chocolate-covered pretzels can have twenty grams of sugar. Yogurt with fruit on the bottom, which many people believe is healthy, can have twenty-six grams of sugar per serving. Often, we are getting all our sugar for the day in only one or two snack foods. When you consider how easily we can consume a yogurt between breakfast and lunch, have a snack bar between lunch and dinner, and then eat a candy bar at the movies at night, it is easy to see how many calories we are putting in our bodies from sugar alone. And this is just from snack foods! Items such as ketchup, barbecue sauce, tomato sauce, and breads that you might have with your regular meals usually have added sugars as well.

SALT

Salt is a mineral that is needed by the body for a variety of different functions. The mineral sodium is present in salt. Sodium plays a role in the body's balance of water and other liquids in the body and blood cells. It also helps with muscle contraction, heart rhythm, and nerve impulses. The human body cannot manufacture sodium, so we naturally crave foods that contain salt to get what our body needs. Throughout history, the human tongue has developed very sensitive salt receptors so we would know when we came upon a food with the essential minerals needed for survival.

Today, processed snack foods are loaded with salt, or sodium, as it is commonly listed. It is often added to improve the taste of many snacks. It is also used in many snack foods simply as a preservative to aid in increasing the shelf life. Potato chips, corn puffs, corn chips, peanuts, pretzels, salsa, beef jerky, and crackers all have very high sodium content. Many common snack foods that you would not think are salty at all can contain sodium, too. Pudding, donuts, chocolate, ketchup, black licorice, and bagels all contain sodium, sometimes far higher than one might expect from a simple snack food.

This excessive salt content in snack foods can have terrible effects on the body. Too much salt or sodium in our bodies on a consistent basis upsets the body's natural balance of fluids and electrolytes. This imbalance can cause us to develop diseases and conditions such as hypertension, osteoporosis, stomach ulcers, heart disease, kidney stones, and kidney damage. Hypertension left unchecked can lead to heart attack and stroke.

Our bodies will either use the sodium in salt or dispose of it in our waste. We are not, however, designed to handle excess amounts of sodium. The healthy human body actually needs only about 200 milligrams of sodium daily. It cannot use more than this, and the excess must be removed from the body by the kidneys. The US Food and Drug Administration recommends about 2,400 milligrams daily, while the American Heart Association recommends sodium be limited to fewer than 1,500 milligrams per day. On average, we consume about 2.5 teaspoons a day or an alarmingly high 6,000 milligrams! That is more than twenty times what the body requires.

At this rate, our bodies cannot get rid of the salt fast enough, and it builds up in our systems. Fluid imbalances, water retention,

WEIGHT ISSUES

There is a difference between being overweight and obese. While being overweight can cause some problems, it is not the major health risk that being obese is. To be obese, a person has to have a body mass index (BMI) over thirty. To be overweight, your BMI is between twenty-five and twenty-nine. BMI is calculated by comparing your weight and height. However, it is important to talk to your doctor. BMI is not a perfect measurement and doesn't account for everything. Being a little overweight does not necessarily mean you are unhealthy.

and even weight gain can result, and our blood pressure spikes, too. A spike in blood pressure causes more strain on our veins and heart. The heart has to work harder to pump the blood at a higher rate. Heart attack and stroke can eventually result from this excess pressure, as well as severe kidney damage if it is left untreated.

MARKETING AND ADVERTISING

Food companies have marketed sweet and salty snack foods to kids for decades. While obesity and illnesses related to sugary and salty snacks are still very high, some changes are being made. According to a federal health and nutrition survey, about one-third of all children between the ages of two and nineteen

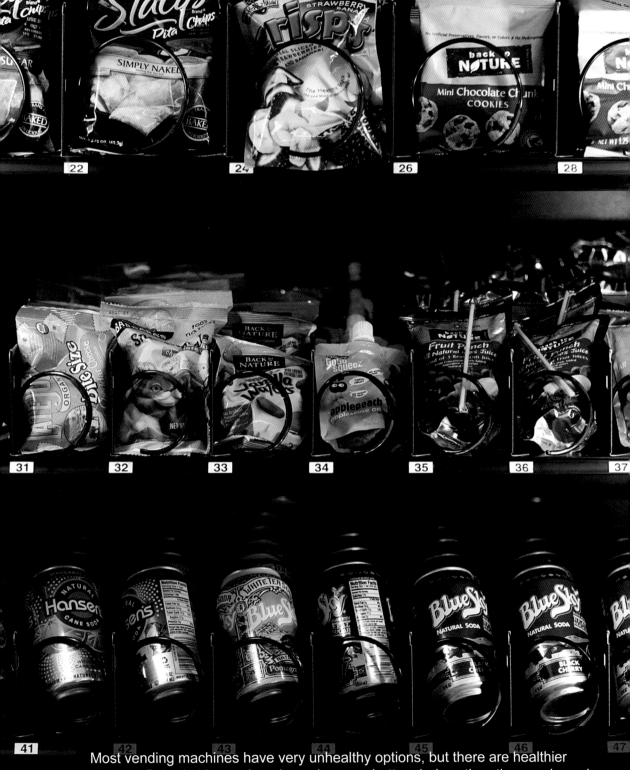

22   24   26   28

31   32   33   34   35   36   37

41   42   43   44   45   46   47

Most vending machines have very unhealthy options, but there are healthier choices. Baked chips and apple wedges are better choices than the usual snacks.

are overweight, and about 17 percent are obese. This is a big increase over the past generation. According to the Centers for Disease Control and Prevention (CDC), in just three decades, the national rate of obesity in Americans has more than doubled. This rate has more than tripled among teens during that same time.

Many parents, students, and teachers alike are fed up with empty-calorie, high-carbohydrate, low-protein snack foods being sold to kids in vending machines, often right in schools. As a result of these unhealthy trends, the Department of Education has new guidelines for what can be sold and marketed to kids. New guidelines would limit available snack food calories to no more than two hundred per serving, keep the sodium content to two hundred milligrams, and added sugars to no more than 35 percent of the total calories. More good news is that the number of high schools and middle schools that sell sugary and salty snacks in vending machines has dropped from 54 percent to 36 percent.

Sugary and salty snacks are treats and should be eaten sparingly. It's fine if you want to occasionally split some candy with a friend or share a bag of popcorn at the movies. Just don't let these snacks become part of your daily diet. If we are careful about what we eat and demand access to healthier snacks like fruits, unsalted nuts, and water or milk, we will see a change in ourselves and our friends.

CHAPTER TWO

SHORT-TERM HEALTH EFFECTS

What we eat has changed drastically over human history. We have gone from hunters and gatherers to having any type of food readily available. And only recently has our food become so processed. Berries and other fruits are some of the sweetest foods in nature. Celery is an example of a natural food that is high in salt. Still, these foods are nowhere near as high in sugar or sodium as many of the processed sugary or salty snacks we eat today.

We crave salty foods because our bodies need sodium to regulate our fluid balance and other systems. We know that we need to eat food in order to have the energy to live and work. Eating more food than necessary helped our ancestors to store fat in their bodies that they could later use when food was scarce. However, the human body can only store so much extra fat

Celery is naturally high in salt and grows fresh out of the ground. It is an unprocessed source of sodium.

before it begins to be negatively affected. Eating too many sugary and salty snacks overwhelms our organs as they try to process all of that extra sugar and salt. Over time, this can negatively affect our overall health.

NOT SO SWEET

When simple sugars are introduced into our bodies in huge quantities and consistently over time, our bodies cannot keep up. The job of your body's pancreas is to produce a chemical hormone called insulin. Insulin is important because it regulates the amount of glucose in your blood. Glucose is a natural sugar that is produced during the digestion process and provides the body with energy. Too much insulin keeps blood sugar levels high, converts more glucose to fat, and does not allow the body to burn some of its stored fat.

With no break between cookies, cakes, pies, or candy day after day, there is no time for fat breakdown to occur. Our bodies keep blindly producing insulin and converting the excess glucose into fat. Regularly eating snacks high in sugar results in energy spikes and crashes. While some initial energy will result from eating a sugary snack, we will then feel sluggish as our bodies work overtime to process the excess sugar into fat.

Erratic sleep patterns can also be a side effect of eating too much sugar. Weight gain is also a serious side effect that results from the body converting sugar into fat. Once the body becomes slightly overweight and poor eating habits are not changed, a person can quickly become seriously overweight or even obese. Obese people have increased risks of high blood pressure, high cholesterol, breathing problems, sleep problems, early arthritis, and even depression.

SALT IN OUR BODIES

With too much excess sodium from salty snacks, your body has to work harder to expel the excess sodium it does not need. The regulation of blood and cell fluids gets out of whack as the body retains more water to compensate for the imbalance. Hypertension, or high blood pressure, can be a serious condition that causes your heart to pump your blood harder, resulting in damage to the cells lining your arteries. Your veins, muscles, kidneys, and heart all must work harder, and your risk of a heart attack increases.

The combination of high blood pressure, caused by too much salt, and insulin problems, caused by too much sugar, makes the body constantly operate in overdrive. Bones and joints become strained from the extra weight. And the body is running at top speed to metabolize sugars and expel excess sodium, even when the body is at rest.

Rather than rarely eating sugary and salty snacks, children and adults alike are now suffering ill effects from consuming these snacks day after day, in addition to their regular meals. Doctors are now seeing an increase in kidney stones in young children, including children as young as eight months old! A kidney stone is a hard mass in the kidney, usually formed from calcium. Doctors think the increase is due to salty foods. When too much salt is consumed, the body reacts by producing excess calcium in the urine. Many of the kidney stones now being found in children have a lot of calcium in them.

Other devastating illnesses and complications arise from eating salty and sugary snacks. With the pancreas working harder than ever to produce insulin, a disease called diabetes can result. Diabetes is a heath disorder that can result when the body can no longer produce enough insulin on its own. When this

KIDNEY ANATOMY

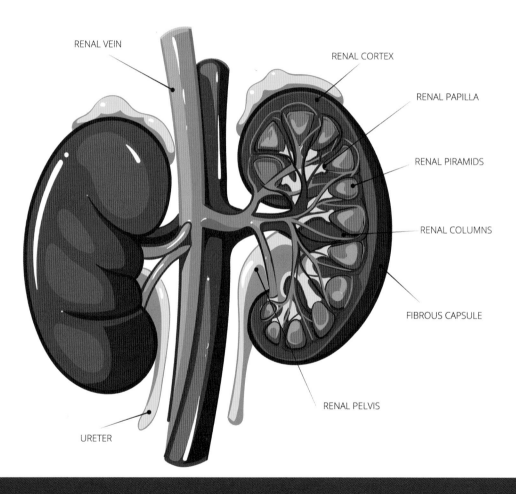

RENAL VEIN

RENAL CORTEX

RENAL PAPILLA

RENAL PIRAMIDS

RENAL COLUMNS

FIBROUS CAPSULE

RENAL PELVIS

URETER

Kidney stones form in the kidney. They are then passed through the body and come out through urination. It can be extremely painful to pass a kidney stone.

happens, our cells cannot absorb glucose well enough to get the energy they need. This is called insulin resistance, and this affects as many as sixty million Americans. Insulin-resistant diabetes can remain undetected for many years. Eventually, though, the body will give up from being overworked.

Broken bones among children have increased in recent years as well. Doctors think this is partially due to an alarming trend of replacing milk with artificially sweetened fruit drinks and sodas.

Disturbing new terms in medicine have emerged due to the overconsumption of these unhealthy sugary and salty snack foods. "Prehypertension" and "prediabetes" are new terms being used to describe high blood pressure and diabetes in young

Milk is full of calcium, which makes our bones strong. Not getting enough calcium can lead to weaker bones that break more easily.

ADDITIVES

When you read the ingredients of a snack food, you might be reassured seeing "natural flavors" or "natural colors" listed. However, natural can mean just about anything. There are many things in nature that you would not want to eat.

Some natural colors are derived from crushed beetles. Natural flavors and colors can also be made from insect secretions, fertilizer, tar, bone char, and many other unappetizing things. Saying natural flavors sounds a lot more appealing than any of those things!

children. Instances of hypertension and diabetes for children are rising at alarming rates. The diabetes most commonly found in children is called type 1 diabetes. But more and more children are developing the type of diabetes usually found in adults, called type 2 diabetes, or adult-onset diabetes. The medical world is now being forced to rename diseases because our unhealthy diets have caused an increase in younger people who become ill.

In order to control diabetes, people must change poor eating habits to good ones, lose excess weight through decreased calorie intake, and possibly take medications. Monitoring one's blood sugar level several times a day is a difficult step to staying healthy. To do this, a diabetic person must prick his or her finger or arm with a sharp needle to draw a small amount of blood.

The blood is then tested with a meter to see if glucose levels are acceptable. This can be an unpleasant process for many diabetic patients, especially children.

Many common snack foods, such as potato chips, cookies, breakfast tarts, cream-filled sponge cake, cupcakes, donuts, pretzels, candy, ice cream, and gummy fruit snacks are all poor snack choices. The excess sugars, artificial or otherwise, and salt or sodium in these snacks are not what our bodies need to stay healthy. Consistently poor snacking habits will result in short-term negative effects, but if not changed, they can lead to devastating long-term health issues that will result in a lifetime of disease and obesity—and can even cause premature death.

CHAPTER THREE

LONG-TERM HEALTH EFFECTS

E ating a bag of chips as a snack or having some cookies after school does not sound harmful. Many of the health effects of unhealthy eating aren't immediately noticeable. Even as a young adult, you may not become overweight or see any obvious adverse effects from the sugary and salty snacks you eat. Your body may have no problem metabolizing that mega-large tub of cake frosting or that giant bag of salty corn chips. But over a lifetime of eating snacks that clog arteries, interfere with blood flow, and organ functions, your body may turn as unhealthy and gross as the snack aisle in the grocery store.

Beyond the short-term effects of being overweight, there are also devastating long-term effects of being overweight and indulging in unhealthy snack foods. The body must work hard to carry the extra weight, and if accompanied with a consistently poor diet, the workload on the body's systems becomes too much to handle. The long-term effects are downright devastating to the systems and organs of the body and can result in debilitating diseases. The American Medical Association believes that obesity plays a big role in the premature deaths of 280,000 US citizens every year. According to the Research and Development Corporation and the University of Chicago, "More Americans are obese than smoke, use illegal drugs, or suffer from ailments unrelated to obesity."

An obese child runs the increased risk of carrying poor eating habits into adulthood and staying obese as an adult. This greatly increases the risk of cancer in such a person. Cancer is when cells in the body grow incorrectly and out of control, often with fatal results. The American Cancer Society has determined that obesity increases the risk for cancer of the breasts, ovaries, gall-bladder, prostate, and colon. It is the excess fat cells in the body that aid in the production of excess hormones, which can cause cancer cells to develop.

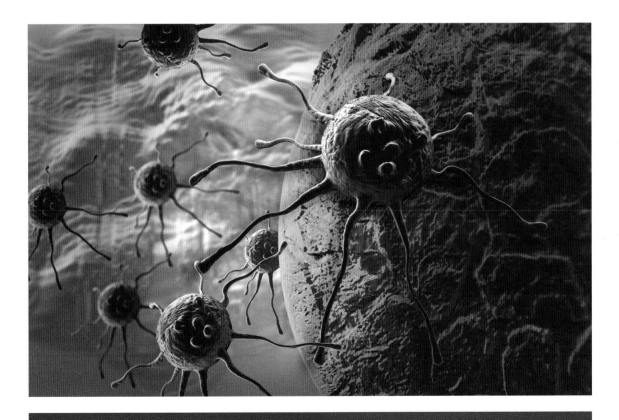

Here you can see cancer cells in the body. There are many causes of cancer, including poor diet and obesity.

SUGAR NOW, SUGAR FOREVER

Evidence and research now shows that childhood obesity may shorten a person's lifespan even if he or she does not remain obese as an adult. The increase in type 2 diabetes in children has a lot to do with obesity. Too much fat on a person's body causes insulin resistance to increase, and the body has a harder time regulating blood sugar. It's a vicious, debilitating cycle in which poor diet causes excess fat. The excess fat increases insulin production, which leads, in turn, to insulin resistance. High glucose levels in the blood destroy the cells that manufacture insulin in the first place. After years of having diabetes, overworked systems in the body break down. Blindness, kidney failure, heart attack, and stroke can also result.

Excess sugar in the limbs of diabetics damages the nerves and can result in numbness and the tendency to become easily bruised. If left unchecked, reduced blood flow greatly increases the chance for infection to develop. As the leg muscles or body extremities are unable to get fuel due to insulin resistance, muscle loss increases. Fat can increase further and cause horrible problems. Some diabetics eventually need to have their legs amputated due to the atrophy that results. Similar problems can happen to the arms. The eyes can also be affected, resulting in blurred or double vision, or even blindness.

Diabetes as a disease is devastating in and of itself. Research has now shown that this disease and the problems associated with it, left uncontrolled, can also aid in the development of high blood pressure, heart attack, and stroke. Higher levels of cholesterol are produced when a person is obese, and this increased fat in the blood eventually clogs arteries. An insulin resistant person's body will produce too much insulin to compensate. The excess insulin causes the liver to produce excess

READING NUTRITION LABELS

Nutrition labels are not as easy to read as they may seem. All packaged food in the United States is required to have a nutrition label that includes the percent of daily value of various nutrients. They are based on a two thousand calorie a day diet. The percentages are also per serving size. At the top of the label, there is a section that says how many servings are in the package. A bag of chips may say that it contains 30 percent of your daily value of sodium but there are three servings in the bag. That means if you eat the whole bag, you'll have eaten 90 percent of the sodium you're supposed to get in a day! Nutrition labels do not include a percentage for sugar. Women should get a maximum of twenty-five grams of sugar per day. For men, it's thirty-eight grams.

fatty acids. High cholesterol can also cause gallstones, which are on the rise for obese children. Excess sodium in a person's diet can also add to this problem.

In women, childhood obesity can result in early menstruation, sometimes before age ten. Irregular or missed menstrual cycles can eventually result from obesity, too. Forty to 60 percent of women who contract cysts on their ovaries in adulthood are also obese.

A SALTY HEART

Increased sodium levels in the body on top of increased glucose levels from poor snack choices will raise a person's blood pressure. The imbalance of fluid regulation by excess sodium causes high blood pressure. According to the American Heart Association, "about 74.5 million people in the United States age twenty and older have high blood pressure, or one in three adults."

Reducing sodium intake to acceptable levels will help lower blood pressure and put less stress on the heart, arteries, and kidneys. When there is too much stress on the body, a person can suffer a heart attack, kidney failure, or a stroke. People with high blood pressure often need to take medication for the rest of their lives to keep their blood pressure under control.

A heart attack happens when blood flow to the heart is blocked or if the heart has a spasm. In overweight people, the heart is working harder. Add high blood pressure and clogged arteries to the already stressed muscle, and it will eventually stop beating. A person's heart is the hardest-working muscle in the body. It constantly beats from before birth until death. When the blood supply that gives energy to the heart muscles is blocked or stopped, a person's heart will stop beating. If the blood to a section of the heart is stopped, even for a few minutes, irreversible cell damage will occur. Depending on the severity of the blockage of blood and the length of time the heart stops beating, a person

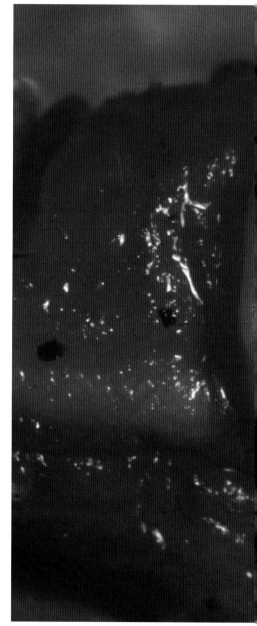

can be killed or severely disabled by a heart attack. Discomfort and pain in the chest, shortness of breath, nausea, dizziness, and pain in the arms, back, neck, jaw, or stomach can all be signs of a heart attack. Experts now think that young people

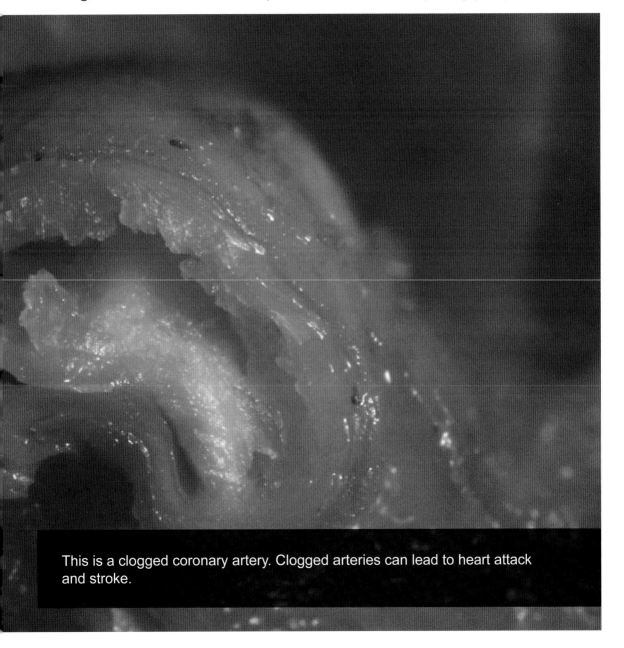

This is a clogged coronary artery. Clogged arteries can lead to heart attack and stroke.

with type 2 diabetes could suffer from ailments such as heart attacks by the time they enter their forties.

Strokes are also related to high blood pressure and diabetes. A stroke is when a blood clot blocks an artery carrying blood to the brain. An artery can also burst. Diabetes, being overweight, and having high blood pressure can all lead to a stroke as the body gets older.

Cancer, diabetes, heart disease, and stroke have now all been linked to a lifetime of poor diets. These diseases are less

Regular check-ups are important to maintaining your health. Your doctor can also answer questions you may have about healthy eating.

common in parts of the world where diets vary from ours and people have a lower consumption of sugary and salty snacks. Living with these ailments can make a person's life miserable and rob us of valuable fun years of healthy living with family and friends. Spending time getting tests, going more frequently to the doctor, and attempting to change deeply ingrained, life-long bad habits is no way to live. So, before you reach for that incredibly salty beef jerky or incredibly sugary toaster pastry, remember that many of these long-term ailments are not easily reversible or even curable.

MYTH

Low-fat snacks are a healthier choice.

FACT

Low-fat snacks are lower in fat, but they are often loaded with sugar. Sugar does not contain fat, but it is converted into fat in the body. Low-fat snacks are not necessarily healthier.

MYTH

We shouldn't eat any sugar or salt.

FACT

When you cook at home, it is fine to add sugar and salt. At home, you can see how much salt and sugar you're adding and not add too much.

MYTH

Once you've made poor diet choices, there's no going back.

FACT

It is always possible to make a healthy change. The sooner the better, as it will be easier to avoid long-term health effects.

CHAPTER FOUR

NO TIME LIKE THE PRESENT

It's perfectly find to treat yourself to a salty or sugary snack once in a while. Problems arise for many people when the special occasion turns into several times a day. Some people even eat snacks in lieu of real traditional meals and have little knowledge about how to snack healthfully.

When we consume too many pretzels, candy, energy bars, potato chips, and cookies, we are then less likely to eat healthy foods that can be beneficial to our bodies. With so many packaged snacks conveniently located for sale in schools, malls, stores, and rest stops, it becomes hard to make the right choice. Many times, there are simply no healthy choices at all, which can be frustrating. But some simple steps can be taken to start new habits. Remember, the time to change is right now. Breaking old, bad habits in favor of new, healthier choices can help you to snack right for the rest of your life.

Bringing healthy snacks with you is a great way to ensure that you won't be tempted by processed, unhealthy snacks.

HEALTHY IDEAS

One way to snack healthfully is to make your own snacks. Sugary snacks, such as banana breads, cakes, cookies, puddings, dried fruit, pretzels, and popcorn, can all be easily made at home from a few basic ingredients. Making these foods from scratch will allow you to control the amount of added sugar and salt. There are also far fewer ingredients than in processed, packaged foods of the same kind.

Making snack foods yourself takes time and is not likely to be something you will do every day. As a result, these treats will be eaten less frequently and on more special occasions. To keep snacks like these fresh and prevent you from overeating, make them in advance, and freeze or refrigerate them at home. Take a few with you before you leave the house in the morning. A couple of cookies as a treat is something that can be eaten between meals only once in a while, not daily.

TEAMWORK

Studies have shown that groups of friends have a huge influence on one another. A study by the *New England Journal of Medicine* showed that the changes of becoming obese increased by 57 percent for those with an obese friend. The opposite is also true. If one friend loses weight, it influences other friends to do so as well. If friends work together to eat healthy and exercise, it may be extremely effective.

When choosing from store-bought snacks, you need to be a detective of sorts to sift through the ingredients label and look for the serving size, added sugars, and sodium content. The serving size will let you know, for example, that if you have huge bag of corn chips in front of you, eleven chips is one serving. It is important to look for this information on a food label. By finding it, you will learn that your big bag of chips should be shared with as many as a dozen people, and that it's not an individual snack size. If you are alone, make sure to take the suggested serving size in a cup or on a plate and not eat directly from the bag, box, or snack food package.

A snack's calorie content is another thing to look for on snack food labels. On average, men and women require only around 1,700 to 2,200 calories a day. There are variations depending on height, weight, age, and activity level. A track runner would require

Moderation is key. A small handful of chips is okay. Moderating your intake can be made easier by putting foods into bowls or onto a plate and only eating that much.

more calories, while someone who has little to no activity would require far fewer. It is important to stay active and balance a healthy diet with activities that will keep the body in shape and keep your heart and metabolism working efficiently. A small snack should be limited to one hundred to two hundred calories, and added sugars and sodium content should also be observed, so you can make sure you are not getting too much sodium or salt for the day. Remember, the USDA recommends only 40 grams a day in added sugars and 2,400 milligrams of sodium.

Above all else, the healthiest foods to snack on are fruits, nuts, and vegetables. Celery and carrots are great portable snack vegetables. With some homemade salsa or ranch dressing, these can be a great snack to eat between meals or when you are on the go. Nuts, such as cashews, walnuts, peanuts, and almonds, are all very healthy snack foods. Remember to buy unsalted nuts whenever possible, or you may be getting too much sodium in one sitting. Some nuts, such as pistachios, come heavily salted and should be avoided except in small quantities. Some nuts also come honey-roasted with a coating

Making food at home from fresh, natural ingredients is the best way to make sure you know what you're eating and that it is healthy.

of added sweetener on them. These, too, are less healthy and should be snacked on in moderation.

Making healthy food choices takes practice. It would be difficult to just wake up one morning and have entirely new eating habits that you are able to stick to. And don't forget that you can still have your favorite not-so-healthy snacks once in a while. Just remember that the rest of the time, you should make an effort to avoid those incredibly unhealthy snacks. You can do it—there are so many reasons to change for the better now!

10 GREAT QUESTIONS
TO ASK A NUTRITIONIST

1. What are some healthy choices I can make when I'm out with friends?

2. What are safe ways to lose weight?

3. How can I avoid salty and sugary snacks in social situations?

4. How can I find out if I'm at risk for diabetes or high blood pressure?

5. Are all artificial sweeteners bad?

6. How important is weight to health?

7. What should I watch out for on nutrition labels?

8. How can I help to get healthier snack choices in my school vending machines?

9. What makes something organic?

10. Are organic snacks healthier?

GLOSSARY

body mass index Weight-to-height ratio used to determine if someone is overweight; also known as BMI.

calorie Unit of heat energy that animals get from food.

cancer Disease caused by abnormal cell division in a certain part of the body.

diabetes Disease in which the body does not produce enough insulin or it cannot process the insulin the body produces.

gallstone Small, hard mass found in a person's gallbladder.

glucose A simple sugar that is needed for energy in living things.

high-fructose corn syrup Corn-based artificial sweetener found in processed foods in replacement of sugar.

hypertension High blood pressure, a condition caused by increased pressure of the blood in the arteries.

insulin Hormone made by the pancreas that regulates how much glucose is in the blood.

obese Above a body weight considered normal; having a BMI above thirty.

overweight Above a body weight considered normal; having a BMI of twenty-five to thirty.

pancreas Gland in the body that helps in digestion by producing insulin.

sodium Chemical element needed by the body to regulate fluids.

stroke A sudden attack caused by an interruption in the blood flow to the brain.

FOR MORE INFORMATION

American Diabetes Association
2451 Crystal Drive, Suite 900
Arlington, VA 22202
(800) 342-2383
Website: http://www.diabetes.org
Facebook: @AmericanDiabetesAssociation
Twitter: @AmDiabetesAssn
The American Diabetes Association provides resources and
    support to people living with diabetes and helps to educate in
    order to prevent people from developing diabetes.

American Heart Association
7272 Greenville Avenue
Dallas, TX 75231
(800) 242-8721
Website: http://www.heart.org
Facebook: @AmericanHeart
Twitter: @American_Heart
YouTube: American Heart Association
The American Heart Association promotes heart health and
    funds research.

Children's Health Foundation
400 West Main Street, Suite 210
Aspen, CO 81611
(888) 920-4750
Email: info@childrenshealthfoundation.net
Website: http://www.childrenshealthfoundation.net
Twitter: @CHACHFPeds
The Children's Health Foundation is a nonprofit organization ded-
    icated to making changes in schools and communities that
    promote health, including prevention of childhood obesity.

Food and Drug Administration (FDA)
10903 New Hampshire Avenue
Silver Spring, MD 20993
(888) 463-6332
Website: http://www.fda.gov
Facebook: @FDA
Twitter: @US_FDA
A division of the United States Department of Health and Human
Services, the FDA is responsible for promoting public health
and supervising the safety of food, drugs, medical devices,
vaccines, and related matters.

Health Canada
Address Locator 0900C2
Ottawa, ON K1A 0K9
Canada
(613) 957-2991
Website: https://www.canada.ca/en/health-canada.html
Facebook: @HealthyCdns, @HealthyFirstNationsandInuit
Twitter: @HealthCanada, @HealthyCdns
A branch of the Canadian government, Health Canada provides
information about food, nutrition, healthy living, the health
care system, and related topics to the Canadian public.

National Association for Health and Fitness
10 Kings Mill Court
Albany, NY 12205
(518) 456-1058
Website: http://www.physicalfitness.org
Twitter: @NAHFofficial
Founded in 1979 by the United States President's Council on
Physical Fitness and Sports, this nonprofit organization pro-
motes physical fitness and healthy habits.

School Nutrition Association
120 Waterfront Street, Suite 300
National Harbor, MD 20745
(301) 686-3100
Email: servicecenter@schoolnutrition.org
Website: http://www.schoolnutrition.org
Facebook: @SchoolNutritionAssociation
Twitter: @SchoolLunch
The School Nutrition Association provides education and train-
ing to those interested in advancing the nutrition of school
lunches and providing nutritious meals to children.

WEBSITES

Because of the changing nature of internet links, Rosen Publishing has developed an online list of websites related to the sub-
ject of this book. This site is updated regularly. Please use this
link to access this list:

http://www.rosenlinks.com/FFTT/Snack

FOR FURTHER READING

Clark, Rosalyn. *Why We Eat Healthy Foods*. Minneapolis, MN: Lerner Publications, 2018.

Gold, Rozanne. *Eat Fresh Food: Awesome Recipes for Teen Chefs*. New York, NY: Bloomsbury USA, 2009.

Kessler, David. *Your Food Is Fooling You: How Your Brain Is Hijacked by Sugar, Fat, and Salt*. New York, NY: Roaring Brook Press, 2012.

Klepeis, Alicia. *Fruits and Vegetables Explained* (Distinctions in Nature). New York, NY: Cavendish Square Publishing, 2017.

Lee, Sally. *Healthy Snacks, Healthy You!* Mankato, MN: Capstone Press, 2012.

Nestle, Marion. *What to Eat*. New York, NY: North Point Press, 2010.

Pollan, Michael. *The Omnivore's Dilemma: The Secrets Behind What You Eat* (Young Readers Edition). New York, NY: Penguin, 2009.

Reinke, Beth Bence. *Healthy Snacks* (Healthy Eating with myPlate). Mankato, MN: The Childs World, 2014.

Sjonger, Rebecca. *On a Mission for Good Nutrition!* New York, NY: Crabtree Publishing Company, 2016.

Ventura, Marne. *Nutrition Myths, Busted!* North Mankato, MN: 12-Story Library, 2017.

BIBLIOGRAPHY

Bakalar, Nicholas. "Fructose-Sweetened Beverages Linked to Heart Risks." *New York Times*, April 23, 2009. http://www.nytimes.com/2009/04/23/health/23sugar.html?mcubz=2&_r=0.

Critser, Greg. *Fat Land: How Americans Became the Fattest People in the World*. New York, NY: Houghton Mifflin Company, 2003.

Hodgen, Donald A. "Global Snack Food Industry Trends." All Business, July 1, 2004. http://www.allbusiness.com/retail-trade/food-beverage-stores-specialty-food/202589-1.html.

Iasevoli, Brenda. "A Plan to Cut Sugar in Schools." *Time for Kids*, February 10, 2004.

Kolata, Gina. "Study Says Obesity Can Be Contagious." *New York Times*, July 25, 2007. http://www.nytimes.com/2007/07/25/health/25cnd-fat.html.

Mayo Clinic Staff. "Artificial Sweeteners and Other Sugar Substitutes." Mayo Clinic. Retrieved June 15, 2017. http://www.mayoclinic.org/healthy-lifestyle/nutrition-and-healthy-eating/in-depth/artificial-sweeteners/art-20046936.

Medina, Jennifer. "In Schools, New Rules on Snacks for Sale." *New York Times*, October 7, 2009. http://www.nytimes.com/2009/10/07/nyregion/07contract.html.

Okie, Susan. *Fed Up!: Winning the War Against Childhood Obesity*. Washington, DC: Joseph Henry Press, 2005.

Poirot, Carolyn. "High-Fructose Corn Syrup Fueling Obesity Epidemic, Doctors Say." *Seattle Times*, December 3, 2005. http://www.seattletimes.com/seattle-news/health/high-fructose-corn-syrup-fueling-obesity-epidemic-doctors-say.

Pollan, Michael. *In Defense of Food*. New York, NY: Penguin, 2008.

Pollan, Michael. *The Omnivore's Dilemma: A Natural History of Four Meals*. New York, NY: Penguin, 2006.

PR Newswire. "Kids Breaking More Bones: Doctors Say Soft

Drinks Poor Substitute for Milk." Goliath Business Knowledge on Demand, March 23, 2004.

Schlosser, Eric. *Fast Food Nation*. New York, NY: Harper Perennial, 2002.

Tanner, Lindsey. "Doctors Say Kidney Stones in Kids on the Rise." Associated Press, March 27, 2009. http://www.telegram.com/article/20090327/NEWS/903270348.

Tartamella, Lisa, Elaine Herscher, and Chris Woolston. *Generation Extra Large: Rescuing Our Children from the Epidemic of Obesity*. New York, NY: Basic Books, 2004.

RSC Advancing Chemical Sciences. "Why Do We Need Salt?" Retrieved December 21, 2009. http://www.rsc.org/Chemsoc/Chembytes/HotTopics/Salt/whysalt.asp.

Zinczenko, David, and Matt Goulding. *Eat This, Not That!* New York, NY: Rodale Press, 2010.

INDEX

ABOUT THE AUTHORS

Julia J. Quinlan is a Massachusetts-based author, journalist, and editor. She has written numerous children's books on topics ranging from honey badgers to plate tectonics.

Adam Furgang has been writing for Rosen for several years. He is an artist, writer, and photographer who lives in upstate New York with his wife and two sons.

PHOTO CREDITS

1/2 3/ 25